LIFE IN A SWAMP

A Wetlands Habitat

Vivien Marais

The Rosen Publishing Group's
PowerKids Press™
New York

Published in 2009 by The Rosen Publishing Group, Inc.
29 East 21st Street, New York, NY 10010

Book Design: Daniel Hosek

Photo Credits: Cover © Tom Antos/Shutterstock; pp. 2–3, 4, 6, 8–9, 10, 12, 14, 16–17, 18, 20, 22–23, 24
© Angelo Girabaldi/Shutterstock; pp. 5, 17 (otter) © Ryhor M. Zasinets/Shutterstock; p. 7 © Cameron Cross/
Shutterstock; p. 11 © Cindy Haggerty/Shutterstock; p. 13 (top) © Clear View Stock/Shutterstock; pp. 13
(bottom), 17(snake) © Rusty Dodson/Shutterstock; p. 15 © Patrick Hermans/Shutterstock; p. 15 (inset) ©
Michal Kram/Shutterstock; p. 16 (bog) © Thierry Maffeis/Shutterstock; p. 16 (marsh) © Slowfish/Shutterstock;
p. 16 (swamp) © Aleksander Bolbot/Shutterstock; p. 17 (dragonfly) © Vnlit/Shutterstock; p. 17 (butterfly) ©
Cathy Keifer/Shutterstock; p. 17 (pitcher plant) © Sandra Caldwell/Shutterstock; p. 17 (moss) © Basel101658
Shutterstock; p. 17 (marsh rabbit, pepperbush, buttonbush) courtesy Wikimedia Commons; p. 17 (frog) ©
Trufero/Shutterstock; p. 17 (blue-winged duck) © Norman Bateman/Shutterstock; p. 17 (yellow-eyed grass) ©
Sony Ho/Shutterstock; p. 17 (water lily) © Motorolka/Shutterstock; p. 17 (deer) © Mike Rogal/Shutterstock; p.
17 (raccoon) © Bob Blanchard/Shutterstock; p. 17 (turtle) © Michael Woodruff/Shutterstock; p. 17 (cypress
trees) © LightScribe/Shutterstock; p. 17 (skunk cabbage) © Paula Cobleigh/Shutterstock; p. 19 © Paul S.
Wolf/Shutterstock; p. 21 (bottom) © Leighton Photography & Imaging/Shutterstock; p. 21 (top) © Lars
Christensen/Shutterstock.

Library of Congress Cataloging-in-Publication Data

Marais, Vivien.
  Life in a swamp : a wetlands habitat / Vivien Marais.
      p. cm. — (Real life readers)
  Includes index.
  ISBN: 978-1-4358-0141-7
  6-pack ISBN: 978-1-4358-0142-4
  ISBN 978-1-4358-2972-5 (library binding)
  1. Swamp animals—Juvenile literature. 2. Swamp plants—Juvenile literature. 3. Swamp ecology—
Juvenile literature. 4. Swamps—Juvenile literature. I. Title.
  QL114.5M37 2009
  578.768--dc22
                                    2008036787

Manufactured in the United States of America

Contents

What Is a Habitat?

A habitat is a natural place where plants and animals live. For plants, it's the area where they grow. For animals, it's where they have their home and gather their food.

Different living things have different needs. Plants and animals of a certain habitat live there because it provides what they need to live. The plants and animals of a habitat, together with the air, soil, and weather, form an **ecosystem** that operates as a community.

A swamp is one kind of habitat. It belongs to a class of habitats called wetlands. Swamps have land and water features that provide a rich **environment** for the plants and animals that live in them.

Water collects in the low-lying ground of swamps. There is also thick plant growth. Many different kinds of animal life find these conditions ideal.

5

What Is a Wetland?

A wetland is an area of land that has water in or near the surface of the ground for at least part of the year. Scientists group wetlands by the types of plant life that grow in them.

Wetlands that have mostly trees and **shrubs** are called swamps.

Wetlands that grow only grasses, **reeds**, and similar kinds of plants are called marshes.

Some wetlands, called bogs, are covered by moss. They have soft, spongy soil called peat that's made of rotted plants.

Most wetlands, including the ones we'll look at in this book, are a combination of swamps, marshes, and bogs.

Swamps have trees and other types of woody plants.

Three Large Swamps

We'll look at three large swamps in the United States. All three swamps are located in the southeastern part of the country, so they don't have long periods of very cold weather. We'll read about the land and water conditions in the swamps and how the plants and animals that live there depend on each other.

Great Dismal (DIHZ-muhl) Swamp is located in southeastern Virginia and northeastern North Carolina. You'll find Okefenokee (oh-kuh-fuh-NOH-kee) Swamp in southeastern Georgia and northeastern Florida. The Everglades are in southern Florida.

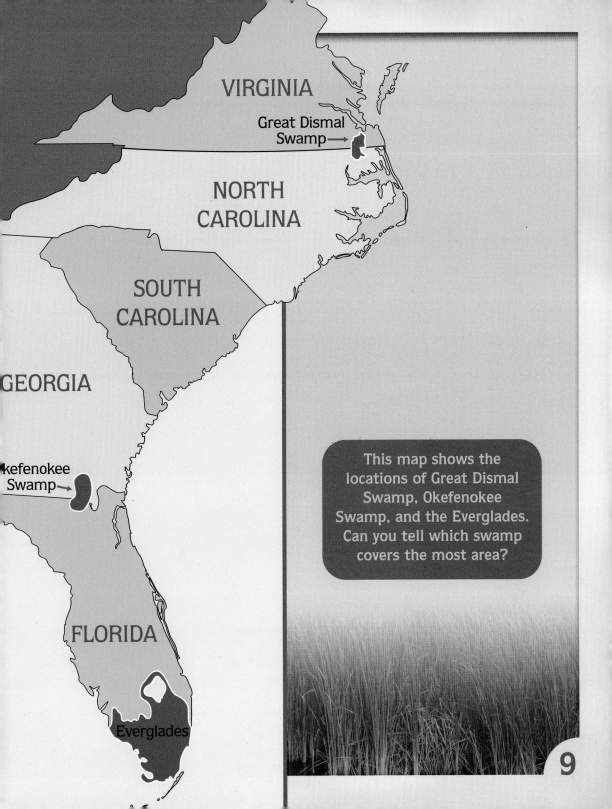

VIRGINIA

Great Dismal
Swamp →

NORTH
CAROLINA

SOUTH
CAROLINA

GEORGIA

kefenokee
Swamp →

FLORIDA

Everglades

This map shows the locations of Great Dismal Swamp, Okefenokee Swamp, and the Everglades. Can you tell which swamp covers the most area?

Life in Great Dismal Swamp

Great Dismal Swamp has many different kinds of plant and animal life. Over 100 years ago, many of the trees in the swamp were cut down. This changed life in the swamp. Today, part of the swamp is a national wildlife **refuge** and is slowly returning to its natural state.

Great Dismal Swamp has plentiful forests of pine, cedar, maple, and **bald cypress** trees. These forests provide homes for more than 200 different kinds of birds, such as woodpeckers, blackbirds, and owls. Squirrels, foxes, bobcats, black bears, deer, and raccoons also make their homes in the forests.

Great Dismal Swamp has one of the largest populations of black bears in the eastern United States.

In addition to its forests, Great Dismal Swamp also has many water habitats. Frogs, turtles, lizards, fish, and over twenty different kinds of snakes make their homes in the water and among the plants that grow there. These animals are a plentiful food source for each other as well as animals of the forests.

In order to return the swamp to its original condition and increase the kinds of plant and animal life, people control the water flow in the swamp and burn certain areas of **vegetation** to create a healthy habitat for native plants.

The cottonmouth snake, or water moccasin, and water skink both live in Great Dismal Swamp. Can you guess how the cottonmouth got its name?

cottonmouth snake

water skink

13

Life in Okefenokee Swamp

Okefenokee Swamp is one of the oldest and largest freshwater swamps in North America. The swamp's name comes from Native Americans and means "trembling earth." Native Americans gave it this name because a large part of the swamp is a bog where the ground shakes when walked on.

Okefenokee Swamp has many different kinds of plants—tiny water plants, flowers, tall grasses, and huge trees. It has bogs, marshes, and swamps.

Over 400 types of birds and animals make their homes in the swamp. The animals range from the smallest bugs and frogs, to different-sized birds such as woodpeckers, owls, and cranes, to the largest alligators and black bears. These animals of the swamp depend on its vegetation for places to live, hide, and search for food.

Visitors use this wooden walkway to view plant and animal life in Okefenokee Swamp. The pitcher plant (inset) is a swamp plant with a sweet liquid that draws insects down into it. The plant then eats the insects!

pitcher plant

15

Okefenokee Swamp:

HABITAT

BOG

MARSH

SWAMP

Habitats, Animals, and Plants

ANIMALS	PLANTS

Life in the Everglades

The Everglades, located in southern Florida, are the most famous wetlands in the United States and also the largest of the three swamps featured in this book. The Everglades are sometimes called th River of Grass. The marsh grasses there grow so close together that they look as if they are in motion in the slow-moving water.

Because the Everglades have both salt water and freshwater, they provide an environment for some unusual and surprising plant and animal life. Everglade plants include **mangrove**, pine, oak, and bald cypress trees, as well as many shrubs, mosses, grasses, floating plants, flowers, and vines.

Cypress trees like the one pictured here have huge trunks, roots, and "knees." Cypress trees breathe through their "knees"!

knees

The Everglades' animal life is as mixed as its plant life. It is the only place on Earth where alligators and crocodiles live side by side.

The Everglades are home to thousands of birds such as eagles, herons, pelicans, and hawks. Frogs, turtles, fish, insects, and snakes are plentiful. Larger animals such as deer, bobcats, panthers, and black bears can also be found. Living in the coastal waters of the Everglades are shrimp, stingrays, dolphins, **manatees**, and sharks.

There are hundreds of separate habitats in the Everglades that provide rich natural environments for the plant and animal life found in them.

The easiest way to tell the difference between a crocodile and an alligator is by the shape of its snout, or nose. Crocodiles have long, pointed snouts. Alligators have broader, more rounded snouts.

crocodile

alligator

21

Wetlands Habitat

We know wetlands are communities of plants and animals that depend on each other and their environment to live and grow. Can you think of other words and ideas you can add to the chart below to help you understand more about wetlands?

Definition
An area of land that has water in or near the surface of the ground for at least part of the year.

Characteristics
- standing water
- grasses, shrubs, and trees that can grow in wet soil

Wetland

Examples
- swamps
- marshes
- bogs

Not Examples
- desert
- mountain forest

Glossary

bald cypress (BAHLD SY-pruhs) A tall tree that grows in swamps. Its leaves look like scales and fall off in autumn.

ecosystem (EE-koh-sihs-tuhm) A community of living things and their surroundings.

environment (ihn-VY-ruhn-muhnt) All the living things and conditions of a place.

manatee (MAN-uh-tee) A large plant-eating animal that lives in the water but breathes air and has hair on its body.

mangrove (MAHN-grohv) A type of tree that grows along coasts in ocean water and has roots that reach down from the branches.

reed (REED) A tall grass that grows in wet areas.

refuge (REH-fyooj) A place set aside to keep plants and animals safe.

shrub (SHRUB) A bush.

vegetation (veh-juh-TAY-shun) Plants.

Index

A
alligators, 14, 20

B
bald cypress trees, 10,
 18
bog(s), 6, 14, 16, 22

C
crocodiles, 20

E
ecosystem, 4
environment(s), 4,
 18, 20, 22
Everglades, 8, 18, 20

F
Florida, 8, 18
forests, 10, 12
freshwater, 14, 18

G
Georgia, 8
grasses, 6, 14, 18, 22
Great Dismal Swamp,
 8, 10, 12

M
manatees, 20
mangrove trees, 18
marsh(es), 6, 14, 16,
 18, 22
moss(es), 6, 18

N
Native Americans, 14
North America, 14
North Carolina, 8

O
Okefenokee Swamp,
 8, 14, 16

R
reeds, 6
River of Grass, 18

S
salt water, 18
shrubs, 6, 18, 22

T
trees, 6, 10, 14, 18,
 22

U
United States, 8, 18

V
Virginia, 8

W
wildlife refuge, 10